TIME SPACE AND DRUMS PART EIGHT

BASIC LATIN
DRUMMING
Foundation

TIME SPACE AND DRUMS PART EIGHT

BASIC LATIN DRUMMING Foundation

DISCOVER OTHER WORLDS

The Time Space & Drums Series
A Complete Program of Lessons in Professional, Contemporary Rock, and Jazz Drumming Styles.

Written and Developed By:
Stephen Hawkins

Graphic Design By: Nathaniel Dasco.
Special Thanks To Linda Drouin and Ikhide Oshoma

ThinkeLife Publications

Time Space and Drums Copyright 2021 By Stephen Hawkins.

All Rights Reserved.

No part of this book may be reproduced in any form or by any electronic or mechanical means including information storage and retrieval means without permission in writing from the author.

The only exception is by a reviewer, who may quote short excerpts in a review.

Stephen Hawkins – Time Space and Drums
Visit my website at www.timespaceanddrums.com

First printing: Jan 2021.

ISBN: 978 1 913929 07 7

Dedicated to the late Paul Daniels and family, Martin Daniels, Trevor Daniels, Paul Mellor's, Keith Richards, Peter Windle, Andrew Marple's, Colin Keys, Peters & Lee, Susan Maughan, Ronnie Dukes, Tom O'Connor, Les Dennis, the late Bob Monkhouse, Bobby Davro, Tommy Bruce, Robert Young, Sandie Gold as well as the hundreds of other people who have played a part in my life experience. Including Sphinx Entertainment, E & B Productions as well as the hundreds of fantastic personalities I have had the pleasure of working alongside over the past 35 years. Apologies for anyone I have missed, not forgetting the current reader who I hope will receive as much from their drumming as I have and more – Stephen Hawkins.

Table of Contents

DRUM ROLL, PLEASE! INTRODUCTION 1

Lesson 1: The Samba Beat 5

Lesson 2: 2, 3 Clave & 3, 2 Clave 8

Lesson 3: Clave Variation Played on Toms 11

Lesson 4: Tango, Cha Cha, Rumba & Bolero 14

    Discover Other Worlds 18

    RUDIMENTARY 19

More Advanced Rolls 19

The 5, 7, and 9-Stroke Rolls 21

An additional Consideration 22

    Featured Drummer Recommendations 24

Worth A Mention 25

Conclusion 25

DRUM ROLL, PLEASE!

INTRODUCTION

Latin drumming is probably the most complex area of drumming—from my own perspective at least. That isn't to say that any other area is less complex, but the basic foundation for Latin drumming at first looks quite advanced, yet is only a starting point, as opposed to $1/8^{th}$ note or $1/4$ note rhythms and even $1/16^{th}$ note rhythms. In particular, the Samba beat is composed of a variation of $1/16^{th}$ note patterns as you will discover shortly.

I won't go into it here but I believe my somewhat aversion to it is based on the fact that in the UK, anything other than the basics covered here is rare at best. So, what they say about fish holds true here also that you can only grow to the size your environment allows. Or, it's rare to see large fish in small ponds and similar. But in the end, this was an err in my own judgment, and if I wanted to pursue Latin drumming more than I did then perhaps I should have moved to a different pond, so to speak. But I didn't and am happy to own that decision. I digress…

These patterns can also have a bit of a twist to them. They may be played or rather felt $1/8^{th}$ note behind, or $1/8^{th}$ note before the actual beat. Or $1/16^{th}$ before or after the beat. This gives the rhythms a spice of life not usually encountered in basic rock rhythms and although basic rock rhythms can be played with the same technique, this tends to make them verge on the contemporary rather than the rock feel.

Please don't get confused here as I don't literally mean playing behind or in front of the beat. I am referring to the feel of the songs and especially the bass line.

Playing in front or behind the beat though is a valid technique that goes beyond the scope of this program. The idea can be very interesting and you should really check out Dave Weckl's videos which contain examples that are far more instructive than I could ever hope to demonstrate here.

Anyway, these rhythms, like any other, become easier the more they're practiced. So, it's best we just get practicing and have some fun along the way with these very interesting rhythms.

I will first, briefly go over the contents then I will give some underlying advice and tips and basic information about the intention of this particular course part plus other useful information you can use as your drumming skills develop. Not forgetting the essence email available by registering for the free audio demonstration of course.

The Time Space and Drums' Basic Latin Drumming Foundation Course includes just four Latin drumming lessons, designed to take the complete beginner through a process that builds a solid Latin drumming foundation. It will also help the intermediate student drummer enhance his/her skills through more focused development and improvement or workout practice.

Along with learning how to play basic Latin drum rhythms, the student will begin to learn the fundamentals of flow, flavor, and variety within one's own playing. Therefore, that student will emerge with a fully rounded basic Latin drumming foundation, as well as having a more enhanced music reading foundation.

Most advanced Latin drumming concepts are built on and from these vital fundamental skills and so, this eighth book forms a basic Latin drumming foundation for the beginning student to build on later.

So, first things first; this is not supposed to be an in-depth look at Latin drumming. This is simply a basic foundation that will allow the drummer to play the most common Latin rhythms in their most basic forms. But keep in mind that those forms can be greatly enhanced by adopting the dynamic playing techniques you would have learned through book 7.

This part is really all about developing the samba beat; simply because the samba will be the most used Latin rhythm you will play along with variations and interpretations of it.

This really allows the drummer to add some flavor to his or her playing as these rhythms are very strongly reliant on dynamics after the scientific mathematical exercise is mastered.

This beat also opens the door much wider to help you sing the types of rhythms I sang in the Dynamics Accents book 7 demonstrations.

Again, we see that this, and part 7, are closely related in their application. More aptly put, these two parts lend an integration that will allow more dynamic use of accents and drum beats in general covered in book 1 and even in book 2. This in most part is due to the flow that the samba bass drum part inspires or portrays.

Regarding the various flavors of music genre, you should ask yourself which world you live in and what your musical surroundings are.

The main issue as a drummer living in the UK, for instance, is that I personally never really attained the experience through constantly playing exotic rhythms such as the sambas, songo beats, and rhythms and to a large extent, general fusion or jazz style drumming.

These styles of drumming really belong in and come from other worlds. Other ponds so to speak. So, if you are into more complex drumming such as Latin, jazz, and or fusion, the UK circuit is probably not the best pond for you to be swimming in.

Take a look at your surroundings to clearly see and then ask yourself, "Which world do I live in?" Other things to ask yourself include: what kind of world you live in and the drumming most appropriate for that world? What are you surrounded by? And of course, which world do you want to live in in the future?

To a great extent, the world that you live in will either limit the type of music you could possibly get involved in or it could help you to progress within a certain genre. And of course, you can always examine other worlds and make a move into those worlds if you are ambitious enough regarding a particular style of drumming that you want to play.

Back to the point. Before you begin these exercises, I leave you with another bit of advice or guidance regarding basic Latin drumming.

Apart from the obvious, learn as many Latin-style drum rhythms as you can, based on searching and finding other written examples of Latin rhythms that we may have not covered in the Time Space and Drums part 8 book... Remember, this is just the foundational first step and a good place to start building on this foundation is to first take advantage of the wiki page below.

https://en.wikipedia.org/wiki/Clave

As you progress through this foundational information in book 8, try to at the very least get an excellent understanding of the samba beat. Learning its flow, flavor, and feel will be of tremendous help as you progress as a drummer, especially in the Latin drumming arena.

It will help you get a better feel for $1/16^{th}$ note fills and solo-type rhythms, especially when incorporated with dynamic playing techniques covered in part 7.

Also, along with mastering the RH cymbal variations here, try to really master the $1/16^{th}$ note patterns played with and without accents on the SD or even the toms. Try accenting each of the $1/16^{th}$ notes until you come up with accented combinations you really like.

Master the ones you're particularly attracted to and find appealing.

So, without further ado, let us begin.

Stephen J. Hawkins

Free Audio Demonstrations

You should visit the following URL to download audio demonstrations of every exercise in this book as soon as possible. You will then receive additional tips and guidance through the included essence emails.

www.timespaceanddrums.com/tsd-8bl.html

Lesson 1

The Samba Beat

The Samba Beat is one of the most enjoyable rhythms to play. I think it's because of the satisfaction one feels when you have mastered it. Not to say that it is overly difficult, but the independence of each limb must be studied and applied with the most scrutinizing eye you have. Further advancement with samba-style beats would be unthinkable without a basic mastery of the rhythms that follow. That said, let's get down to work. You never know, you might get it straight away.

Play the RH on the ride cymbal bell for this one. As you can see, it's a variation between 1/16th notes as well as 8th notes.

Exercises 1

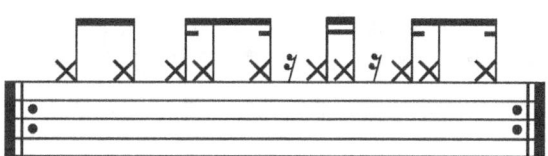

Exercises 2

Now add the left foot HH on beats 1, 2, 3, and 4.

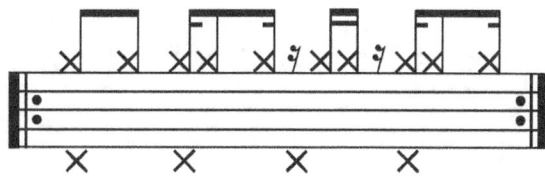

Exercises 3

When you're ready, you can add the samba bass drum pattern with your RF.

Time Space and Drums DISCOVER OTHER WORLDS

Make sure you are comfortable with this rhythm before going any further as it can cause trouble later if you don't absolutely nail the bass drum. Play as slow as you need to in order to get everything in.

Exercises 4

Now add the SD.

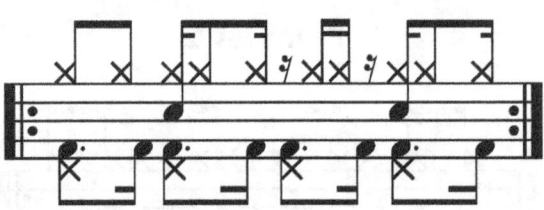

Exercises 5

This time, try playing the HH using the left foot on the "&" of each beat. Start with the RH cymbal bell again.

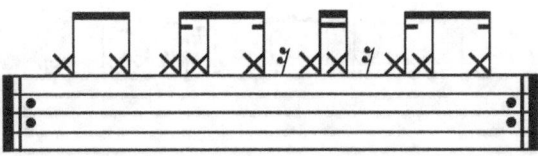

Exercises 6

Now add the offbeat HH pattern.

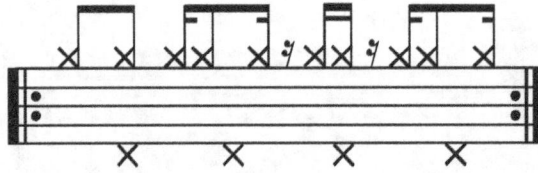

Stephen Hawkins

Time Space and Drums   DISCOVER OTHER WORLDS

Exercises 7

Now add the samba BD pattern. Should you have any problems with this exercise, I would suggest playing just the feet together, then add the LH. When you are comfortable with these three limbs, you should work the RH pattern in slowly.

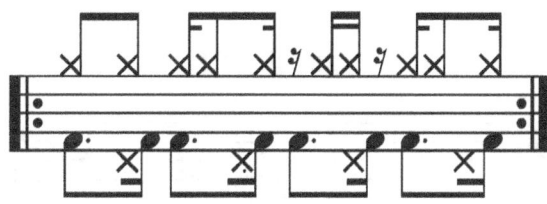

Exercises 8

Now add the SD.

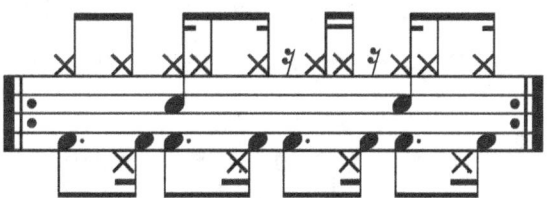

I hardly need to say it but if you are a complete beginner then you should not progress until you absolutely nail these first exercises. Thankfully, when you have control over these exercises, you have basically completed the whole book. It doesn't get much harder than that. Well, not just yet anyway.

Time Space and Drums   DISCOVER OTHER WORLDS

Lesson 2

2, 3 Clave & 3, 2 Clave

Only when you have mastered the last samba beat should you continue with the next exercise which is a 2, 3 clave samba. Begin by playing the LH pattern as in exercise 1.

Exercises 1

Exercises 2

Now just play the RH pattern. As you play this pattern, imagine how the LH fits this rhythm. Visualize the pattern in the exact place it should be. Visualize each note in its place. Then attempt to put them together in exercise 4 with the LF playing 1, 2, 3, and 4.

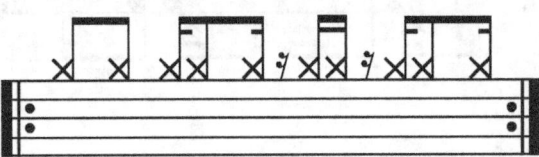

Exercises 3

Now play the LF HH.

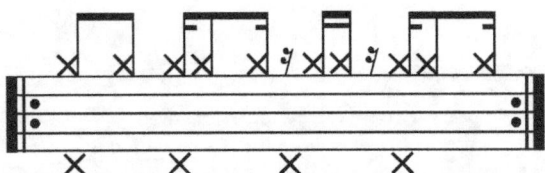

Exercises 4

Now attempt to put the RH, LH, and LF together. If you have any problems, try slowing the tempo right down. Dissect the rhythm until you can play all three parts.

Stephen Hawkins

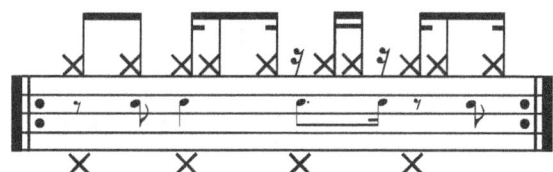

Exercises 5

Now try adding the RH pattern. Again, if you have any problems, try dissecting the rhythm until you can piece the rhythm together.

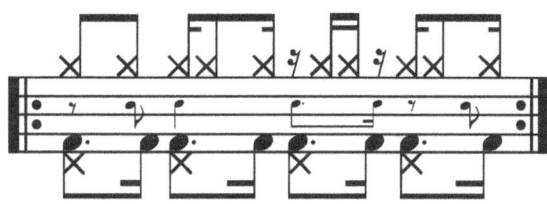

THE 3, 2 CLAVE

Exercises 6

Now try the LH pattern the opposite way round to the 3, 2 clave.

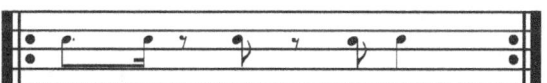

Exercises 7

This time, play the RH pattern and visualize where the 3, 2 clave notes fit. Make sure you have a good idea of where the parts fit together.

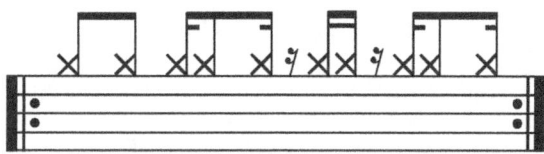

Exercises 8

While still visualizing where the notes fit together, try playing the LF HH pattern.

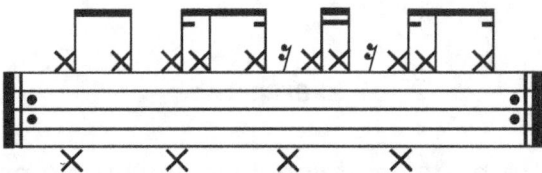

Exercises 9

Now attempt to piece it all together.

Again, dissect the rhythm until you can play it.

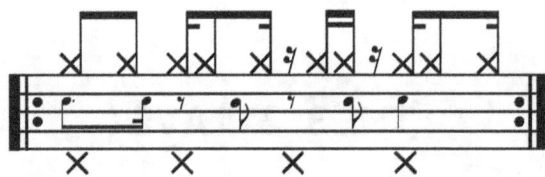

Exercises 10

Now add the BD pattern. Dissect it if you have any problems.

Lesson 3

Clave Variation Played on Toms

Before we try a variation, try playing these SD patterns over the samba BD.

Exercises 1

The sticking here is RLRL, etc.

Exercises 2

Now try playing a paradiddle over the samba bass drum.

Exercises 3

This time, accent the first of each group of paradiddles.

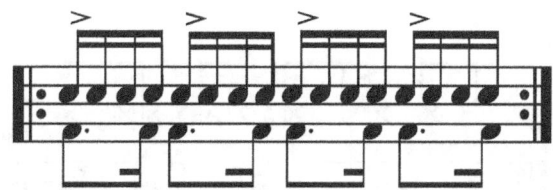

Samba Variation

Exercises 4

Play the RH samba pattern.

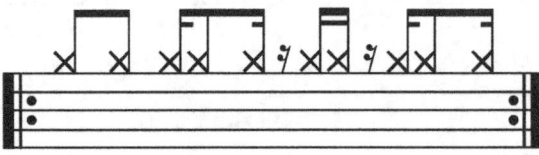

Exercises 5

Now add the LF HH.

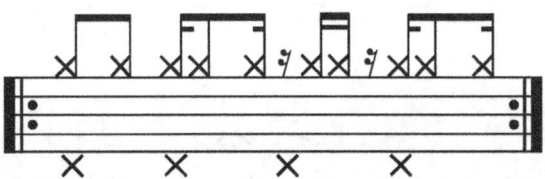

Exercises 6

Now try this 3, 3, clave pattern.

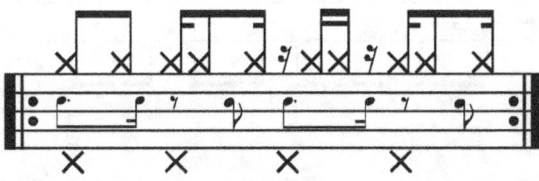

Exercises 7

Now add the BD.

Exercises 8

When you feel comfortable with the last exercise, try playing the LH pattern around your three toms.

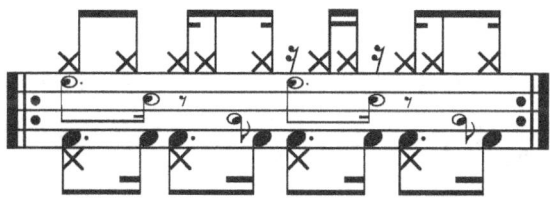

Variations Cymbal Patterns

Exercises 9

Try these variation cymbal patterns with the 2, 3 clave. You could also use the 3, 2 clave.

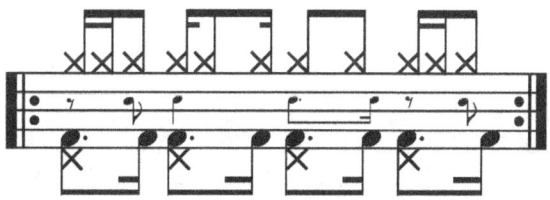

Exercises 10

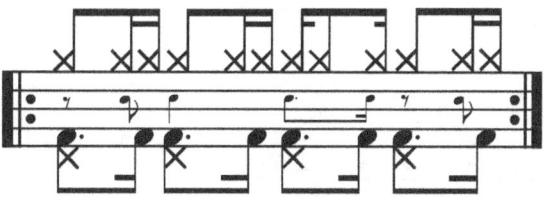

Exercises 11

Lesson 4

Tango, Cha Cha, Rumba & Bolero

The following Latin rhythms are a little less tricky than the samba. First, try this tango rhythm. The sticking is R, L, R, L, etc.

Exercises 1

Exercises 2

Now add this closed roll.

Exercises 3

Now try this 1/8th note roll.

Exercises 4

Now try this 1/8th note roll as a double stroke roll.

Time Space and Drums   DISCOVER OTHER WORLDS

Exercises 5

This time, play a rock beat style BD pattern.

Cha Cha.

Now let's try some cha-cha rhythms.

Exercises 6

Exercises 7

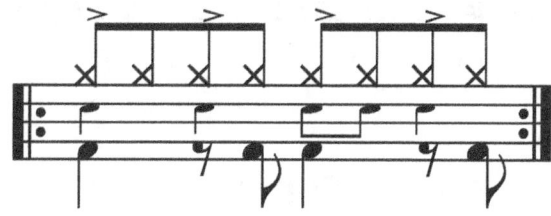

Stephen Hawkins

Exercises 8

Exercises 9

Exercises 10

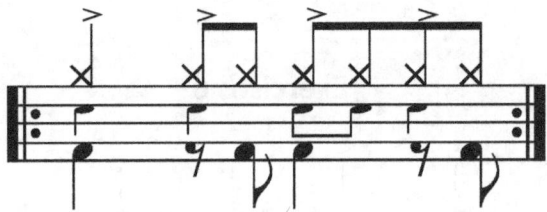

Exercises 11

Rumba

Try this rumba using the toms.

Exercises 12

Exercises 13

Now add the BD pattern.

Exercises 14

Now play the rumba around the toms.

Bolero

This is a very interesting rhythm called the bolero. You may recall Torvill & Dean with their ice-skating dance; the music used was by RAVEL.

Exercises 15

Discover Other Worlds

Well, as before, the title *Discovering Other Worlds* is another metaphor that implies different planetary worlds. Of course, the worlds we are speaking of in our analogy are the worlds as in Latin beats. These can be divided into several worlds such as Reggae, Cuban, and general Latin and so on, which are all really styles or genres.

But the metaphoric universe is more of a playful one than it is an exacting science but you knew that right?

Nevertheless, each particular world has its own various little nuances in terms of drumming, to quite a large degree. This is again more about feel than anything else but from a practical point of view, there are subtle and not so subtle changes within the rhythms of these worlds or genres that make the style of drumming completely separate from rock or jazz style drumming. But remember we are integrating the various styles here and not dividing them.

For example, in Reggae, the bass drum is often played on 2 and 4 as opposed to 1 and 3. Other Latin-style beats and rhythms displace the bass drum pattern in a variety of other ways in such a way that the bass drum pattern becomes the focal point to create a better flowing rhythm.

Yet others still remain close to the standard rock style beats or straight ahead 4/4 style beats.

RUDIMENTARY

More Advanced Rolls

As mentioned in book 7 in the Time Space and Drums series, single strokes and double strokes make up most of the other rudiments or are integrated within other rudiments in one way or another.

That was obviously the case with the paradiddle (RLRR, LRLL) and it is somewhat obvious in the rolls that follow.

As I have done within previous books, I will refrain from showing the way that these rolls are written and instead describe the sticking and processes. I believe that doing it this way will allow a deeper understanding of the movements that are required to perform the exercises or rolls. If you want to see the written exercises in notation form, please visit timespaceanddrums.com as they are available in the member's area free of charge.

The rolls that follow differ from the rudiments that we have covered; in every rudiment we have covered so far, there was an endless or continuous rhythm or flow. Once you learned the paradiddle, single stroke roll, double stroke roll triplets, and buzz roll, you played the sticking pattern in an endless loop of $1/8^{th}$, $1/16^{th}$, or, as suggested earlier, $1/32^{nd}$ notes. But of course, in an actual playing situation, you would simply play the rudiment within rhythms and beats as well as fills and phrases.

The flam was slightly different as, by its very construction, it was a short rudiment which is generally played within other rudiments be they single strokes, double strokes, paradiddle, triplets or another pattern.

The rolls that follow are identical to double stroke rolls with a minor exception—they all have a specifically designated end. We will cover the 5, 7 and 9-stroke rolls here but it should be borne in mind that these rolls can also be extended to 11, 13, 15, 17-stroke rolls and beyond.

This means that if you start a roll on beat 1 of a bar of 4/4 music and played the roll for just 1 beat, you would essentially have played an 8-stroke roll. But if you ended that roll on beat 2, then the roll becomes a 9-stroke roll.

The observant reader will now recognize that we have doubled the strokes per beat from 2 x 8th notes, 4 x 16th notes, and again to 8 x 32nd notes.
This is how the notation values compare to the 4 1/4 notes or crotchets.

The note values from top to bottom are then:

(1/4) Quarter notes or crotchets.
(1/8th) Eighth notes or quavers.
(1/16th) Sixteenth notes or semiquavers.
(1/32nd) Thirty-second notes or demisemiquavers.

Looking at the chart above clearly shows that as far as time is concerned:

A 5-stroke roll lasts one-half beat and ends on & of the first beat of the bar (1 &).
A 9-stroke roll lasts one whole beat and ends on the second beat of the bar (2).

And the 7-Stroke roll ends on the last 1/16th note of the first beat.

So, the 5-stroke roll begins on the first beat and ends on the third 1/16th note of beat 1. It can then can be repeated on beats 2, 3, and 4 if the drummer wishes to play repetitive 5-stroke rolls in strict time to the 1/4 notes or pulse.

And so, the 7-stroke roll begins on the first beat and ends on the fourth 1/16th note of beat 1. It can be repeated on beats 2, 3, and 4 if the drummer wishes to play repetitive 7-Stroke rolls in strict time to the 1/4 notes or pulse just like the 5-stroke roll.

So finally, the 9-stroke roll begins on the first beat and ends on the fifth 1/16th note or beat 2 and can be repeated again, starting on beat 3. From that, you should be able to see that only two 9-stroke rolls can be played within a bar of 4/4 music. But that can be advanced further. Although, for now, we will stick with making things simple so you get the basic foundational knowledge and theory.

The 5, 7 and 9-stroke Rolls

So now you understand the theory, let's see how you would play the rolls. In particular, let's look at the sticking. We will look at all three rolls together for this.

5-stroke roll sticking:
R R, L L, R

7-stroke roll sticking:
R R, L L, R R, L

9-stroke roll sticking:
R R, L L, R R, L L, R

So, after the explanation of the note values and now with the addition of the sticking, you should be able to see that the count for each roll is something like this:

5-stroke roll count: 1 &.
7-stroke roll count: 1 e & a.
9-stroke roll count: 1 & 2.

Now, I will admit this is the only time in all of the book series that I feel the need for a video demonstration. Simply because if I keep writing the descriptions by adding another level, which is basically already covered but worthy of note. All of the examples begin on the first beat of the bar then end at the relevant place within the beats. The 5-stroke ends on the & or 1, the 7-stroke ends on the "a" of "1 e and a" or the last 1/16th note in a group of 4, and the 9-stroke roll ends on the 2 of 1, 2, 3, 4.

If that isn't clear, please visit the timespaceanddrums.com members area and watch the rudiments demonstration in video 8.

An additional Consideration

To make things even more complex (remember complexity is still a basic fundamental in this particular situation and so I say complex related to the already slightly awkward instruction included here), the above exercises should be practiced as if they were a single stroke in themselves. By that I mean 5-stroke, 7-stroke and 9-stroke rolls. Although they contain 5, 7, and 9 strokes respectively, treat them as if each was just a single stroke. For example:

5-stroke roll:
R R, L L, R is a single stroke.

7-stroke roll:
R R, L L, R R, L is a single stroke.

9-stroke roll:
R R, L L, R R, L L, R is a single stroke.

Each of the strokes is right-hand lead or begins with the right-hand. However, although each roll should be practiced right-hand lead, they should also be practiced leading with the left-hand and so the sticking becomes:

5-stroke roll:
L L, R R, L

7-stroke roll:
L L, R R, L L, R

9-stroke roll:
L L, R R, L L, R R, L

After which, you would practice each of the rolls using alternate sticking patterns like this:

5-stroke roll:

1 & 2 &

R r, L l, R.   L l, R r, L.

7-stroke roll:

1   e   &   a   2   e   &   a
R r, L l, R r, L.   L l, R r, L l, R

9-stroke roll:

1   &   2   3   &   4
R r, L l, R r, L l, R.   L l, R r, L l, R r, L

It is a good idea to practice each of the rolls here without a metronome until you have some degree of mastery over the actual sticking patterns with both left-hand as well as right-hand lead, followed by alternate sticking. Then you may want to try playing them in time to a metronome.

One last consideration is that of movement and motion. Once you get a little flow going and can begin to play the rolls using alternate sticking smoothly, you will again become aware that there is a motion to help you along. The Left-Right motion, in this case, is a regimental one indicating and suggesting a sort of precision and accuracy that you may not have been aware of until now. Either way, try to play these rudiments accurately and precisely as you play the motions from left to right.

Even if you have to slow the tempo just a little, remember that precision is more important than speed.

Featured Drummer Recommendations

Carlos Vega

I hesitate before I include Carlos Vega in this particular book for a couple of reasons. First, he is a drummer I haven't really listened to a lot when it comes to variety but I have listened to him quite a lot with regards to one artist in particular. I am of course referring to Dave Grusin, although you could also include Lee Ritenour here as, to be honest, I always known them as being in the same lineup; hoever, that isn't exactly true.

So, back to Carlos Vega: because I haven't really listened to him a great deal, I can only refer you to Dave Grusin, Lee Ritenour, and the Dave Grusin and GRP All-Stars band, especially the *From The Record Plant* live video if you can find it.

Although the artists mentioned above are not specifically linked to Latin music, they all in most cases add a Latin Funk style to the rhythms and beats. Therefore, I highly recommend having a listen to these artists as they have a mix of Latin and straight-ahead rock and/or jazz feel. To me, these artists are bands for musicians only but of course, that isn't strictly true either.

The bad news about Carlos Vega is that he died in 1998, aged 42 and since the internet has gotten a whole lot bigger since then, there isn't really that much to see when it comes to his latest drumming videos. Also, most recordings are not as good as they would have been today but there is still quite a bit to see if you search online for this awesome drummer.

Latin drumming, from my perspective, is really about creating a variation of the feels that lays somewhere in between jazz and rock. Technically, that isn't the case but as a feel, I tend to prefer that description. Of course, Latin music has a whole new set of rhythms and claves which sets it apart from rock and jazz, but here my rather inadequate explanation of Latin drumming serves simply as a guide. It is here for you to make your own judgments after listening to more Latin drummers, as there are plenty of choices if you do a search online for Latin drummers.

As I mentioned, I hesitated to include Carlos Vega because I personally know little about him, apart from what I have mentioned here. It serves you though to at least check him out for yourself as he really deserves more than I have added in this short section.

Worth A Mention

As this is a short section, I believe that Steve Gadd deserves a mention here; in particular, his recordings of Spain by Chick Corea. Another source of fantastic Latin style rhythms is the pianist, Michel Camilo; in particular, the album titled One More Once. Please be warned that this is really heavy-duty jazz, Latin-oriented music so it's not for the faint of heart. However, if you do like that kind of music, you would most likely love the jazz pianist, Michel Petrucciani, who again plays a lot of Latin-based rhythms in his music and also makes use of the great session drummer like Steve Gadd, Dave Weckl, and others.

And so, that is about the limit of my Latin recommendations as living in the UK, you don't get very close to playing such awesomely exotic rhythms as is required for some of the artists I have mentioned here. But at least this points you in the direction of Carlos Vegas' Latin style rhythms and influences just to get you started.

Conclusion

Congratulations are in order. You have successfully completed the Basic Latin Drumming foundation set of lessons. You have worked very hard and deserve a break. However, I suggest that you spend the next few months working on, and then absolutely mastering what we have covered so far in the series. Write some of your own exercises and work on them. Try some odd-time exercises and play through them too.

You should be an absolute master of what we have covered so far in the series. Don't skip over anything. You should judge yourself with the X factor in mind. Get everything perfect at different tempos and different volumes. If you have any difficulty with the theoretical part, get yourself a good book on music notation and theory and study it. Get everything in the pocket so to speak.

Only when you are the absolute master of the rhythms we've covered so far should you go any further in the series. Be your own instructor and make sure you discipline yourself.

Make sure everything is just right. When it is, move on to the next part of the series: developing creativity.

Until Next Time,

Stephen J. Hawkins

Closing Note:
The Time Space and Drums series is intended as a complete program from Part 1 to Part 12. It is strongly advised that you follow the program in order of the parts as they integrate and build on each other. The only thing I can now add is to practice each exercise until you have them all mastered. Mastery comes from paying attention to the most basic fundamentals already covered in each of the exercises within this book.

Once you have perfected each exercise you may like to try them left-handed but that may take time depending on your current skill level.

Free Audio Demonstrations
Please don't forget to visit the following URL to download audio demonstrations of every exercise in this book as soon as possible. You will then receive soma additional tips and guidance through the included essence emails.

www.timespaceanddrums.com/tsd-8bl.html

What's Next
Thank you for choosing Time Space and Drums as one of your learning tools. I hope you enjoyed the process. You can explore more of the series in Developing Creativity Volume One, the ninth book in the Time Space and Drums Series by searching for "**Coordinated Combinations**" Developing Creativity - Volume 1" at your favorite bookstore.

Share Your Experience
If you have a moment, please review this Rock Drumming Foundation book at the store where you bought it. Help other drummers and tell them why you enjoyed the book or what could be improved. Thank you!

Thank you again dear reader and I hope we meet again between the pages of another book. Remember, You rock!

Other Books by The Author

Modern Drumming Concepts
Rock Drumming Foundation Series part. (Six in-depth Drum Lessons).
Jazz Drumming Foundation Series part. (Six in-depth Drum Lessons).
Rock Drumming Development Series part. (Six in-depth Drum Lessons).
Jazz Drumming Development Series part. (Six in-depth Drum Lessons).
Odd Time Drumming Foundation Series part. (Six in-depth Drum Lessons).
Accents and Phrasing Series part. (Four in-depth Drum Lessons).
Basic Latin Drumming Foundation Series part. (Four in-depth Drum Lessons).

 Have you ever thought about what it would feel like to make a living as a pro drummer?

If so, then visit the Drum Coach website. I might be for YOU!

The purpose of the Drum Coach blog is not only to provide drummers with valuable information but also to help them share their passions.

The Drum Coach provides all types of drumming information from beginner lessons right up to professional level playing skills, as well as personal self*(drummer)*-improvement essentials – there's something here no matter your skill level!

Some of the most important information on this website comes from my personal experiences as a percussionist and musician for over 35 years. So, I invite you to take advantage of the Drum Coach Experience, whose aim is to provide high-quality, on-demand information for drummers as they travel along their journey to achieve their personal drumming goals and ambitions.

Our commitment to our readers is always 100%! If you have any problems, questions, or concerns, just let us know and we'll help you take care of the situation as quickly as possible.

And remember to **Stay In Time!** and continue to **Rock!**

www.ingramcontent.com/pod-product-compliance
Lightning Source LLC
Chambersburg PA
CBHW081358080526
44588CB00016B/2531